What is Therapy?

Duaine Carlton

Order this book online at www.trafford.com
or email orders@trafford.com

Most Trafford titles are also available at major online book retailers.

Note for Librarians: A cataloguing record for this book is available from Library
and Archives Canada at www.collectionscanada.ca/amicus/index-e.html

Printed in Victoria, BC, Canada.

ISBN: 978-1-4269-1443-0 (sc)

*Our mission is to efficiently provide the world's finest, most comprehensive book publishing
service, enabling every author to experience success. To find out how to publish your
book, your way, and have it available worldwide, visit us online at www.trafford.com*

Trafford rev. 8/14/09

www.trafford.com

North America & international
toll-free: 1 888 232 4444 (USA & Canada)
phone: 250 383 6864 ✦ fax: 812 355 4082

Further Resources

AlcoholicsAnonymous
 www.aa.org/lang/en/aasite_finder.cfm?origpag=72
NarcoticsAnonymous
portabletools.na.org/portaltools/MeetingLoc/
Sex Addicts Anonymous www.sexaa.org/
Substance Abuse Treatment
www.samsha.gov/index.aspx
Alanon www.al-anon.alateen.org/meetings/meeting.html
Mental Health of America   www.nmha.org
Crisis Hotlines   www.athealth.com
United Way   www.liveunited.org
Homeless shelter Locator
www.homelessshelterdirectory.org
Catholic Charities community.catholiccharitiesusa.org

Table of Contents

What is Therapy?

Forward

There are many kinds of therapy to help individuals. Occupational Therapy helps people heal from surgeries, strokes and retrains people for life skills and activities of daily living. Physical Therapy helps people to regain physical abilities. Mental Health Therapy which encompasses substance abuse, sex offenders and other criminal behaviors as well as personal issues. When discussing Mental Health, the word "therapy" conjures up as many ideas or perceptions as there are human beings on planet earth or grains of sand on a beach. Some of these perceptions are: lying on a couch, hypnotism, administration of electrical shock, brain surgery, sexual issues and predispositions to sexual desires and believe it or not, the ability to read their minds.

Therapy is a process whereby an individual, client, seeks the services of an individual who is educated through the liberal arts, gains work experience, obtains a license and may or may not, specialize in a specific area of therapy. Therapy relies on the validity and reliability of theories. Theories are derived from many areas of the helping professions such as physicians, pharmacists, occupational and physical therapists, social work, nursing, law enforcement, etc. Theories are ideas, or thoughts, as to why things happen and the resulting consequences. It is then studied whether alterations would produce a productive or non productive outcome.

Throughout my 12 years of being a therapist I have heard many opinions concerning Mental Health Therapy. So the reason I wrote this book was to help you, the reader, better understand therapy. I believe that therapy, as well as therapists, has been misunderstood because our profession cannot produce facts. Some would say that we are not scientists, or that we are not able to provide concrete evidence, like doctors can with x-rays, MRI's or other scans available to them. However, we can, with the MRI's, PET and other scans, see how the brain is functioning. Thus, we can accurately assume that some individuals have a tendency to exhibit certain behaviors. But all in all our profession is predominantly based on what people tell us. As you will read, there are certain instances where we do have facts, however sometimes these facts are provided by people who may have intentions that are not necessarily good ones.

For the purposes of this book, therapy refers to understanding human behavior, thoughts, and actions, in conjunction with the many theories that have been developed, toward others and our own selves. This book was conceptualized and written based upon many past clients' answers to this question: 'Do you know what therapy is?' It has been my personal experience that 98% of individuals either answer "No" or provide an answer based upon what other have told them, or what they may have seen on television and the movies.

It is the hope of this author that you, the reader, will become more educated as to the practice of therapy so that you may seek services for yourself and provide insight as to what therapy is to others. Also that you and others will not be reluctant to seek professional help for situations you may be suffering from or experiencing. Most importantly, it is to correctly answer the question: 'What is therapy?'

Chapter 1
Why Therapy?

Why is therapy necessary and how do you know if you or someone you know should need therapy? I believe the best way to answer this question is with other questions. Why do people go to the doctor? Why do people go to the dentist? Why do people go to the chiropractor? It seems pretty obvious; people experience a physical ailment or medical emergency-a toothache, or backache. Fortunately, we as human beings can feel a physical problem such as back pain or a toothache. When we do, we first try to alleviate the pain with over-the-counter medication, or a home remedy and if that does not work, and as a last resort, we make an appointment with the appropriate professional. Unfortunately there are no warning signs that there may be a problem with our behavior, our thought processes and/or our actions. Unlike illnesses where a person can find over-the-counter remedies, there are no over-the-counter remedies for such problems as mental or behavioral deficiencies. Therefore, the only option is therapy. Have you ever wondered why people seem to take advantage of you? Have you ever wondered why you have had many dates with others and you cannot seem to find that perfect mate? Have you ever wondered why it is difficult for you to make friends? Have you ever wondered why people always seem to be picking on you, or it appears that people are against, or out-to-get you? How about thoughts that "He/She just did that to make me mad", or " Why is it when the family gets together Uncle, or Aunt, so and so always becomes intoxicated, or shows up intoxicated?" or "relative so and so always causes an argument with, or fights with so and so?" If an individual has answered yes to any one of these questions, then he/she may need to seek therapy.

Individuals often ponder the questions posed after they have been exposed to these things or have experienced them first hand. As a result some people develop increasing difficulty in dealing with issues, and they may try to compensate for their problems. Many people are able to deal with their problems in an efficient, effective manner and are able to cope appropriately with everyday life situations. Therefore therapy is not for those individuals, nor for those whom experience severe mental illnesses such as mental retardation or mental illness associated with severe brain injuries.

All of us encounter daily struggles such as difficulty dealing with a boss, co-worker or peers, always running late or falling behind, kids yelling and screaming, having difficulty in school, traffic, not getting what you ordered from the drive-thru, or not having enough time to enjoy life. Most individuals are able to understand and adjust to the daily grind of life without consequences. For example, with problems associated with dealing with others, many of us can say to ourselves, "maybe they are having a bad day" or, "maybe he/she had an accident on their way to work or are experiencing pressure from the boss." Where as, people who are unable to think this way may say, "That person is a jerk," "that person treats everyone like that," or "they do not need to treat me that way, I have never done anything to him/her." Can you see the difference in the comments just presented? The first set of questions consists of conceptualizing what another person may be experiencing and the second implies a personal threat. Being able to understand others does not indicate or imply that we are placing blame onto others. Rather we are, or should be, striving to understand others and the unique situations that they are experiencing outside of our interaction with them.

The discussion so far has focused on the interpersonal conflicts as to the need for therapy. However there is a more devastating reason why others seek therapy, and often times these individuals have created for themselves severe consequences.

There is a larger group of individuals within our society that require therapeutic services. Their pathology may be masked through their behaviors and/or thought processes that help them to get by in life, until one day, or through an inadequate judgment, these aversions are no longer sufficient to effectively manage their psychopathology. The psychopathology I am referring to include people suffering from the group of vast mental illnesses and distorted thought processes. Most individuals with these deficiencies often enter therapy because their interpersonal problems become intrapersonal, that is the internal struggles of the individual become unmanageable and begin to affect others or create difficulty in developing and maintaining relationships with others and with society. Also, individuals may have developed patterns, or cycles, within their life that contribute to the problems already mentioned. Such as, patterns of divorce or unstable, frequent relationships, frequent job loss, frequent altercations with others and law enforcement, disregarding or disrespect for others and their property, numerous failed relationships and/or relationships with abusive partners, reduction in participation of leisure/fun activities or hobbies, isolation from friends or family, etc. Many individuals who experience these and other difficulties do not seek therapy on their own accord. Rather, they are often times referred by others such as courts or probation, physicians, friends or family. More often than not, however, those referred through the legal system fail to comply with therapy. Many people who come to therapy are unwilling to participate or comply with treatment recommendations, because they do not believe they have problems even though they may have experienced numerous episodes of negative consequences. When this happens the therapist should be persistent and encouraging to the patient. Many comments I have heard from individuals who have been referred for therapy include: "I got into an argument with him/her and gave him/her a push and they fell down," or "My physician suggested I see a therapist because he/she thinks I am depressed (or mention any other symptom), but I feel fine now because I am on (Zoloft, Paxil, etc.) now," or " I don't know why they suggested I come here," or "I was driving home, a cop pulled me over, he/she said I was swerving and I was charged with a DUI," or "they found a joint in my car" and the list can go on endlessly. Though these can be legitimate comments, or statements, it has been my professional experience that the behaviors have occurred for a number of months, or years, and the individual has crossed the threshold of self-harm, or threat-to-harm others. It is disconcerting that so many individuals deny, or fail to acknowledge, their deficiency and they allow their behavior to permeate their function and abilities of everyday life before they seek treatment or are referred to treatment.

Therapy allows individuals to talk to someone about their problems without being ridiculed or told to just "get a grip," or to "snap out of it." The unfortunate part is that most individuals believe that they can solve their problems on their own without professional intervention. The reality is that, because we can get so wrapped up in a situation, we become like a deer in the headlights, whereby all we can conceptualize is what we are seeing or experiencing. Most individuals are encouraged to talk to a friend or family member. Though these may be well-intentioned suggestions they may not be very effective for several reasons. The first, what if the friend they are talking with is actually part of the problem? Like most individuals, we will not convey our true feelings for fear of loosing this friend by telling about their problems with shared friend. Second, what if the individual has experienced some trauma at the hands of a dysfunctional family member such as sexual abuse? Research and experience demonstrate the effects of coercion and blackmail dictate that the victim will not communicate with family members, again for fear of offending other family members, or for fear that something bad will happen to someone in their immediate family. Friends and family typically also do not have the expertise to communicate to the psychologically impaired individual and provide the correct method of empathy and compassion concerning the situation. Another important issue to consider is that friends and family are too close to the issue and may be partial or may have strong emotional bonds concerning the individual or the situation. As a result it would be very difficult for a friend or family member to be objective and impartial. Though it is the ideology of our western culture to be an individualist and to work out problems on our own without external influence, I can not help but think about the individual who has a long history of say, substance abuse, to quit without someone else's intervention and help in identifying triggers. But this is the reality of the situation and the purpose of this book is to educate and inform the public about what therapy really is, and to encourage individuals to consider therapy.

Chapter 2
What is Therapy?

Therapy is the utilization of strategies and/or techniques that have been researched through application. The strategies and techniques utilized by psychologists have been used with clients who present with various problems and as the treatment progresses, case notes are written to record successes and failures of the techniques used. As a result of these trials, we now have many models that have been shown to help individuals throughout the years and are still used today. Therapists typically use several different therapies when working with individuals for two important reasons. First, people are individuals, which means I do not think or act like you do and vice versa. Therefore it is imperative that a therapist be well trained in all aspects of therapy and their techniques and applications. Second, in today's world there are many variables that make it very important for the therapist to be aware of and to have a working knowledge of the variables with which they are faced. Such as mixed marriages, both racial and cultural, the various cultures represented in our country, the norms and values of each culture, gang activity, drugs, alcohol, crime, thought processes and behavioral processes of all individuals across the spectrum. A common question in my experience in dealing with individuals who have substance use problems has been "How can you help, or know what it is like to have this problem if you have never used before?" Though this is rational, I personally do not believe that I have to have a substance abuse problem, or any other problem for that matter, to effectively work with individuals and families who do. My response to this way of reasoning is this: "Do you have to be a mechanic to work on a car?," or "Do you have to be a professional lawn care person to do yard work?" and the answer to all these is unequivocally "No." I believe that the difficulties individuals are confronted with are easily understood and comprehended through the ability to listen and not be judgmental of the individual and his/her problems. Maintaining with seminars, networking with other professionals and reading journals are crucial to developing a working knowledge of what effective therapists are involved with on a daily basis.

Therapy is conceptually different than counseling in that counseling is process whereby individuals seek advice. Alternatively, therapy is a process, as mentioned earlier, where individuals strive to make changes through cognitive restructuring and behavioral changes. For example, people who seek counseling services do so for money such as credit and financial planning and career and life planning. Individuals who utilize these services often times have a plan or a direction and need someone to advise them on how to make it work in regards to retirement, job placement, or investments to name a few. Therefore the premise of counseling is to give and get advice. For example, a Career Counselor will implement what are called aptitude tests that will assist an individual who may be looking for a career change or a promotion. Therapy on the other hand does not function as an avenue for giving advice because there is either a physiological or psychological element to the individual's level of functioning, either on a personal or intrapersonal level. Giving advice would be imparting personal beliefs and values that are the therapist's and not necessarily those of the patient. Therapy does not do this because individuals who seek therapy have their own beliefs and values, however their level of functioning has, in some way or another, altered these beliefs and values. We as therapists should strive to help the individual reach their previous level of functioning. The therapist does this by challenging current beliefs and values with previous ones. Therapists try to help individuals understand how their level of functioning is affecting themselves and others through their own accounts or the reports of others. Imparting advice upon the individual by the therapist would be detrimental to the function and purpose of therapy, as well as compromising the thoughts and belief systems of those who already are confused and/or disoriented.

Chapter 3
Group vs. Individual Therapy

Therapy consists of the individual and group process. Both therapies utilize similar therapeutic concepts however they are unique in the approach that they utilize. Individual and group therapy are often done separately but sometimes they are utilized in conjunction with each other. Each therapeutic technique has obvious pros and cons in their ability to help individuals with their problems and they accomplish this in a unique and distinct manner. I will begin by discussing group therapy and conclude with individual therapy and my hope is that you will acquire enough knowledge and understanding that you will be able to recognize the best option for yourself or for a loved one.

Group therapy is very common especially in the community mental health systems and inpatient treatment facilities such as hospitals and specialized treatment facilities that deal mainly with abuse issues and eating disorders. There are some private practitioners who provide group therapy services. Groups are designed specifically for focusing on a specific problem area such as substance abuse, sexual abuse, eating disorders, physical abuse, gambling and, in recent years, borderline personality disorder, DUI offenders, or adolescent first time offenders.

Some individuals consider groups such as Alcoholics Anonymous, Narcotics Anonymous as group therapy. However, they are considered support groups because these and the numerous others like them, allow addicts (addicts are individuals who have developed either a psychological or physiological addiction) to secure a support system and provide accountability for continuous sobriety. Support groups are also available to family members and friends of addicts. A support system is a network of addicts who are available 24 hours a day, 7 days a week to help individuals that are experiencing "urges" to use again and to hold each other accountable for their choices. These support groups also allow individuals to interact with each other and to learn how others who have experienced addiction have learned to abstain from their substance of choice. Often individuals are involved with a substance therapy group at the same time as being involved in a support group. Encouraging participation in a support group in conjunction with therapy is very effective because the individual is continually held responsible for maintaining sobriety. Support groups utilize non-professionals to facilitate these meetings. There are many different kinds of support groups and each one has a specific function. For example, they help people deal with issues like AIDS, grief, survivors of incest and rape, military spouses and family etc.

The therapy group has gained popularity within the past 10 years for two reasons: financial and time. Practitioners who are funded through grants (money allocated by states and the federal government) are encouraged, or more appropriately mandated, to establish group therapy as part of their program. Insurance companies are also mandating, or strongly suggesting, that providers do more group work. The reason is twofold. First, large numbers of individuals can receive treatment at once, thus saving money. These entities suggest that a group consist of no less than 8 and as many as 15 for one therapist and allow for a co-therapist with 16 or more participants. (These figures are approximate due to fluctuations in allocated monies). Second, because of the numbers of individuals receiving treatment at the same time, the length of treatment is significantly reduced.

The large number of individuals participating in group therapy can experience excellent outcomes. They experience a sense of belonging in that others who are in the group have similar problems and experiences thus, providing a sense of not being alone or being different. Most people who have similar problems or life deficiencies have had similar backgrounds, or life experiences. These are shared with others and this can establish cohesion between the therapist and members. Cohesion is essential for the group process to be effective because the members need to believe that they are not alone in their suffering. Also when they hear others' recollections they are more willing to disclose their own unique stories. This disclosure contributes to another key attribute of group therapy and that is accountability.

Accountability is a process where the individual is held responsible for his/her behaviors and actions instead of blaming others or circumstances for their behavior. Accountability then reduces the level of an individual's denial of a problem and the blaming of others for their life problems. Obtaining responsibility for their own behaviors is a major accomplishment as well as a fundamental step toward treatment success. This is accomplished when the therapist or group members confront the individual and challenge previous disclosures or instances of irrational thinking.

Group therapy can be short term or long term depending on several factors such as who is recommending treatment, the offense for which treatment is recommended and whether this is a first time offense, or the facility where the service is being provided. As mentioned earlier, there are a number of facilities where group therapy is offered, from inpatient (hospitals, prisons, clinics etc.) to numerous outpatient ones (private practice, community mental health centers, hospitals, half-way houses etc.). Often the length of treatment is determined by where the service is being provided. For example, if an individual was admitted to a hospital, the treatment can last a week or longer depending on the circumstances for which the individual was admitted (suicide attempt, drug overdose etc.). If treatment is recommended by the legal system for a DUI, sexual assault, mediation, or something else, the treatment time frame can also be variable.

Short term group therapy can be done either inpatient or outpatient. With short term therapy, they are commonly referred to as "cookie cutter" programs whereby they follow a strict regime of treatment guidelines and manuals and time sequence. Because of time constraints, participants do not have the opportunity to discuss in detail their unique situations as those in individual therapy do. This is very important to allow participants the freedom to communicate what they are thinking and feeling because these emotions may be more important than working through the modules and completing the worksheets. Individuals progress through stages, usually in a workbook format, where they complete worksheets after a module is discussed and then at the next meeting they discuss their homework assignments. When all participants have completed the modules, or workbooks, they are evaluated by the therapeutic team on such criteria as participation and assignment completion, and then the recommendation for graduation is made.

Short term group therapy is extremely popular because it is less of a financial liability for insurance companies and programs funded by government entities. Examples of short term therapy are EAP's, Employee Assistance Programs and Solution Focused Therapy. EAP's are provided to employees of companies that have mental health benefits through major insurance companies such as Magellan, Blue/Cross Blue Shield, etc. This is not to say that they are ineffective, rather they have several shortcomings pertaining to the quality of treatment that is offered to those participating. The premise is that short term group therapy is effective because several individuals are being serviced at the same time and the money spent to treat them is significantly less.

Long term group therapy helps clients develop stability and prevents a higher level of treatment. Long term group therapy can also be conducted in either an outpatient or inpatient facility it is often done in specialized clinics or private practice. Usually the therapists who are working in these facilities are specially trained in a specific area or domain. Unlike short term therapy, long term group therapy is more precise and targeted to specific populations based upon age, gender and the problem area. Long term group therapy utilizes a screening process to eliminate individuals who do not present with the same problem area. As mentioned earlier, the purpose of a group is to offer treatment for a large number of individuals who present with similar problem areas, thus the purpose of the screening process. The screening of an individual for a group consists of more than just the presenting problem. It considers the individuals' willingness to interact with others and whether their cognitive ability will allow them to understand and comprehend the group process.

The long term group therapy process follows a similar treatment plan in that the participants work in workbooks and progress through stages. The main difference is that the participants are receiving better and more focused treatment. With long term therapy there is ample time to allow for participant input, to ask questions and to become more involved with their treatment. As mentioned earlier, this is very important for the participants to be allowed to discuss issues that may be important to them because these same issues or comments may be important to someone else in the group. Also long term therapy helps the client to develop stability and may prevent the need for a higher level of treatment such as hospitalization.

The main objective in group therapy is to get the participants to accept responsibility for their behaviors and actions and the most effective manner for this to occur is allowing participants to interact and talk with each other. Remember that the purpose of a group is to reduce denial and to do this an individual needs to be confronted by others. This is the central theme to group therapy. Without participants having to be held accountable for what they have done and said then this cannot be accomplished.

Even though group therapy is very effective common within mental health, not all individuals are good candidates for groups. Some people are not comfortable talking in front of others while some may view group therapy as a breach of confidentiality. Some individuals may be cognitively challenged or have certain psychopathologies which are not suitable for group participation. That is why we have individual therapy.

Individual therapy has long been the standard within psychology since the early 20th Century and remains, in my professional opinion, the most effective mode of treatment. Individual therapy, like group therapy, has many disadvantages.

Two main disadvantages are that only the individual and the therapist are involved in the treatment process, and secondly, it is difficult for the therapist on his/her own to hold the individual accountable for their own behavior, due to the one on one interaction. Though these present obstacles toward the treatment process, they can be dealt with effectively.

Individual, or one on one therapy, is just that-the therapist and the client. Though to many this arrangement would be considered a disadvantage, it is a benefit for both the therapist and the individual. It is beneficial in that the therapist can focus on the client and the associated problems and issues instead of dealing with many problems at once. For the client, he/she knows that they are working with one therapist and has that therapist all to themselves and does not have to share time with others. The client also has the benefit of revealing information in a more secure setting reducing fears or complications associated with confidentiality. Most individuals entering therapy generally have information to conceal that they are more willing to discuss when only one person is present especially when they consider their personal issues embarrassing. The individual still may be apprehensive about revealing some information, but as the sessions continue and he/she becomes more confident in the therapist, they will eventually talk more freely. The therapeutic bond that occurs between the therapist and the client is much more difficult to make and maintain in a group setting. This bond is directly related to trust and confidentiality. When the majority of individuals enter into therapy, they are generally concerned about their current life situation and want to change. The exception is those who are referred through the legal system and are generally more defiant and resistant to the treatment process. However, this is a subject too broad and will have to be reserved for another book.

Individual and group therapies are the means to treatment for all individuals and the therapy chosen is dependent upon the individual, the problem and the recommendation of the referral source. Other factors include: the available resources within the individuals living environment and the insurance company, which may or may not provide therapeutic coverage. Individual and group therapies are the kinds of therapies offered, but within these two modes there are a variety of methods, which are utilized in helping the individual to become a more productive person.

You may be thinking "How do I determine if group or individual therapy is what I need?" The following is a guide to help you decide which one may be more appropriate for you:

1. Are you more comfortable talking with one person, or do you prefer to interact with others?
2. Are you someone who likes to talk, or do you prefer to listen to others and talk occasionally?
3. Do you feel that 1 hour would be more appropriate, or do you feel you need 2 or more hours?
4. Do you want others to know about you and why you are in therapy, or do you prefer that fewer people know?
5. Would you prefer having access to a professional therapist or do you prefer a non-professional?
6. Do you have a diagnosis that may not allow you participation in a group setting? In this instance a licensed professional may be most helpful in choosing individual or group therapy.

Individual Therapy	Group Therapy
Client and therapist	Less than 8 clients – One therapist
Working with one person	More than 8 clients – Two Therapists
Encourages Family and Significant other	Working with several people at once
Involvement	Open or Closed Sessions
More problem focused and goal directed	Discussion and confrontational
Therapist is viewed as the expert	Clients usually have different problems
Session management is easier	Clients see others views
Expensive	Therapy can be disorganized
Sessions are usually 1 hour	Sessions can be 2 hours or longer
Assessments, treatment plans and testing	Placed in a group by a therapist
Private Practice or Community Mental Health	Community Mental Health or Support Group Oriented

The methods, called theories, are what the therapist considers when doing therapy with individuals. Though there are many ways of doing therapy, they are categorized into 8 different theoretical perspectives pertaining to how and why individuals have regressed and/or progressed to their current state of functioning. These are Psychoanalytic, Adlerian, Existential, Gestalt, Behavior and Cognitive, Christian Therapy. Some of these have been combined because they utilize similar concepts and ideas, but for the focus of this book and to avoid confusion, I will discuss each as a separate therapy.

Chapter 4
Psychoanalytic Therapy

Probably the most recognized yet most understood method of treatment that has been in existence since the early 20th Century is Psychoanalysis. Psychoanalysis was founded by a former physician turned psychologist, Dr. Sigmund Freud. He hypothesized that his clients were suffering from episodes of hysteria. These clients, when questioned about their childhoods, began to recall that there were significant past episodes which were sexual in nature-both what they had experienced and their inner thoughts concerning sexuality. From these verbal recollections and utilization of associations to unlock repressed memories, psychoanalysis focused on primitive and repressed thoughts of the mind. Along with this aspect came the hypothesis that individuals were always battling the forces of the mind that influenced immediate gratification versus delaying the gratification. Psychoanalysis also hypothesized that individuals were driven by self-constructive desires as well as self-destructive desires. In other words, people are dealing with a battle between a thriving living force and a death or destructive force.

The most controversial aspect of psychoanalysis was the gender of the individual and how gender contributed to an individuals' neurosis. Most of the individuals who were clients during this time period were females. In part because the social climate of that time considered the female gender to be less superior to their male counterparts; therefore the female was most frequently referred to therapy. This may account for the emphasis, and hypothesis, that emotional distress was directly related to the females' subconscious wish to be male. Though the hypothesis that gender was responsible, or at least partially responsible for psychopathology, psychoanalysis has pretty much abandoned this assumption and is no longer the main force driving it. Instead psychoanalysis continues to focus on an individual's earliest recollection of childhood and from there begins therapy.

Psychoanalysis is traditionally reserved for the individual setting due to the unraveling and retracing of an individual's life. As a result of this extensive life history and the methods utilized to help the individual understand it, psychoanalysis is an extremely long term therapy, for which many insurance companies are not willing to compensate. The psychoanalytic method is still in place, however it is more likely conducted in large urban areas and is paid for privately.

Chapter 5
Adlerian Therapy

Alfred Adler worked with Freud however Adler believed that psychological deficiencies were socially influenced, instead of biologically as Freud believed, and that the individual was functioning at his/her best according to which social interactions in which they lived. Adler believed that individuals were motivated by societal influences and constraints and were merely wanting to satisfy their own desires through any means necessary and to whatever their interaction with society would offer to meet their wishes, or desires that needed to be met. For example, an Adlerian therapist may assume that a person who commits an act directed towards society is not having his/her needs met. Therefore, to get what it is that he/she needs, or requires, from society he/she is behaving in a manner to have a need, or needs, met. The Adlerian therapist may be interested in helping their client process why he/she may be motivated to participate in those things that have contributed to his/her situation. In doing so, the therapist may also explore what the client is expecting to achieve by engaging in certain behaviors as well.

The Adlerina therapist with this information may be able to help him/her think about their actions as being harmful towards society and the common good. Thus, altering his/her thoughts from a self serving one to thought processes that are beneficial to obtaining what it is he/she needs as well as a more positive person within society. Personally, I would consider Adler the first psychologist to accept the idea that individuals are products of their environments-a concept associated with Social Learning, which will be discussed later.

Adlerian therapy assumes that individuals are motivated by social factors and operating within these social factors. The individual is working to achieve some goal or goals. With this in mind, the individual is seeking to establish, or find, his/her identity and to fit in with society somehow. With this theology, therapists who utilize Adlerian therapy do not view individuals as suffering from abnormal personality, rather they believe that the individual is functioning at a level that promotes personal growth, integrity and character and has a continuous search for some significance within the societal structure in which he/she is living. Therefore, the Adlerian therapist would imply that he/she needs to become involved with various organizations to find his/her purpose within society while at the same time promoting a better society. Some organizations that come to mind are, M.A.D.D, S.A.D.D, YMCA, YWCA, Girl Scouts and Boy Scouts to name only a few.

The focus of Adlerian therapy is to help the individual work towards changing mistaken notions, teaching individuals better ways to meet daily life struggles, providing direction, and offering encouragement to individuals who feel discouraged and hopelessness in their life. The goal within Adlerian therapy is to assume that the individual is functioning at his/her best within the confines of their social preference, and that they are seeking to find significance and meaning as well as, reaching an intended goal for which the behaviors and actions help to achieve.

Chapter 6
Existential Therapy

Existentialists, as these therapists like to call themselves, focus on the assumption that individuals have the freedom to choose how they make sense of their lives, instead of biological, psychological and social processes determining how individuals live their lives. Unlike the biological, psychological and social therapies, existential therapy believes that even though we are free thinkers and no other process affects our ability to think and make choices, we and only we are responsible for our own actions and behaviors. Therefore we alone are the so-called "architects" of our lives. Individuals are not considered to be the victim of circumstances, or being in the wrong place at the wrong time, rather we choose to be where we are and do what we do without regards to any other external influence. Essentially the individual is striving to find values and a meaning to life through his/her views or experiences in their lives thus far.

Existential therapy assumes that individuals have the ability to make good choices concerning their lives. Therefore, one of the goals to this particular therapy is for the individual to be challenged concerning their current values and meaning and discover new ones through alternative ways of problem solving. Based upon my professional experience, there has been very few times in which this method has worked for me. I believe that an individual has to have a good understanding concerning where they want their life to go as well as, have the ability to conceptualize a plan to obtain their desired goal. Existentialist therapy is considered as a "New Age" concept and that there is no right or wrong in the choices he/she makes. Rather it focuses on what he/she considers to be the force behind his/her meaning of life. In my opinion, Existentialism is a fancy term for liberalism, or to coin a phrase from the 60's and 70's, "If it feels good do it."

Chapter 7
Behavioral and Cognitive Therapy

Behavior therapy utilizes both the behavior and cognitive theories as well as relying on research. Behavioral therapy attempts to alter, or elicit behavioral changes while at the same time replacing irrational thought patterns that may or may not be contributing to such behaviors. Behaviorists believe that individuals adopt, or learn, behaviors from our environment whether it is from our family of origin, peers, or through other means. Individuals can develop behaviors in many different ways. This includes influences from different forms of media (T.V, books, radio), playing, watching others' behaviors within various situations and their social reactions from others (acceptance or rejection), individual feelings and emotions after the behavior was exhibited (gratification, release of anger, or pleasure etc.) and interactions with others (how do others interact with the individual?) etc. However the ability to discern which behaviors are inappropriate can be difficult because there are many different ideas as to which behaviors are appropriate and which are not. This is based upon several factors such as the person's culture, social economic status, geographical location, living environment, and expectations-both personal and societal.

The cognitive aspects of behavioral therapy focus on such things as irrational thoughts, cognitive level of functioning, views and belief system orientation and formation, thought processing (internal or external), biological and environmental contributors and / or causes, chronological age of the individual(s) etc.

As mentioned earlier, behavior and cognitive therapies involve research. The studies are conducted in a variety of ways such as personal interviews, interviews of others, questionnaires, surveys, observations, case histories, MRI's, CT scans, PET scans etc. Research is an excellent resource in being able to predict and suppress behaviors, however, there are several variables that need to be considered and obviously can not be predicted nor identified. As a result, many individuals believe that behavioral and cognitive therapy is not beneficial to a long term benefit. However the effects of both behavioral and cognitive therapy on individuals, just as with any other therapy utilized is dependent not only on the individual, but also on environmental and biological determinants.

Personally and professionally, I utilize both the Cognitive and Behavioral therapeutic concepts and ideas because I believe that we are products of our environments, social makeup, family of origin and highly susceptible to societal influences. Also, it would be difficult to change behavior patterns without addressing cognitions as well.

Chapter 8
Gestalt Therapy

Gestalt therapy originated in Germany with "Gestalt" meaning "the sum of its' parts". An individual was assumed to have some aspect of himself/herself not functioning in sync with the rest of the organism. The therapist views the individual as consisting of a network of psychological processes which are not functioning as one unit, or whole entity. For example, to some people an orange is just that, an orange. However, a Gestalt therapist would see the orange as not just a whole orange but, just a part of what the orange really is and that is the seed, the juice, the pulp, individual slices, the inner skin, the core, the outside skin and the color.

Individuals who are involved with Gestalt therapy, are encouraged to look for support within themselves and to be aware of all the experiences they are feeling in the current moment as well as, recognizing the cognitive processes or the emotional responses which are suppressing the individuals awareness to such experiences being felt at the time. With this theology, individuals are supposedly responsible for their actions and behaviors and they can deal with the many problems, or situations that they face on a daily basis. As a result, the individual is expected to determine their psychological deficiencies and find ways within themselves to correct them on their own. In this manner, the therapist is merely a guide to help the individual rely more on self support through internal processes of emotions and reactions rather than external support for acceptance of these emotions and feelings by challenging individuals to work through the cognitive challenges so that they can regain control of themselves, challenging the individual to accept they are not realizing their cognitive awareness and to decide if they are willing to make the necessary adjustments to become aware, be in the moment and to create situational scenarios which will allow the individual to access their internal awareness.

Chapter 9
Christian Therapy

Until now, the previous chapters have discussed therapy from a scientific, almost factual, perspective based on research and observation, but mostly from personal opinion. Personally, I have to confess that I fell hook line and sinker for those theories previously mentioned. I did this for the better part of 7 years into my career.

Personally, I accepted Jesus as my personal savior and became baptized at the age of 19 {1979} and like most "new" Christians, I reverted back to my previous ways of living. I realize now that I did not have a mentor to guide me in my spiritual walk. Then 19 years later, 1998 to be exact, all that changed. I met my wife and she re-introduced me to Christ, the one who had touched me many years prior. Since that time, in 1998, God has convicted my heart in such a dramatic fashion that I began to question my many years of education as well as the way I viewed my profession and conducted therapy. I was not receiving the satisfaction from my work that I should be experiencing. Also, God has blessed me with countless mentors, not only in peer relationships, but also in personal ones. I would like to thank Stan, my spiritual brother, for his encouragement and fellowship since we first met in 1999.

One of the first things I had to accept was that all were created by God and are to be used for His glory and kingdom, not for my personal and selfish desires. The second thing that really got my attention was that we humans rely on the following three things:

1} Our family of origin, 2} Our own thoughts and beliefs and 3} On what the world, or society, teaches us.

The previous three things I have mentioned are what I consider to be the basis for the theories that have been presented thus far. For example, Psychoanalytic Theory says that our problems are a combination of our upbringing and innate {things we are born with that are not influenced by anything else} makeup. Rogerian Theory says that we are unchangeable and that we are functioning the best we can because we do not know any other way, based upon circumstances. Adlerian Theory says that we know what is best for us and that we need to have guidance, or assurance, that we will achieve what it is we want. Gestalt Theory says that psychological problems are the result of some psychological malfunction that makes up the complete individual. Existential Theory says that the individual is responsible for finding the help he/she needs thru an individual experience, whatever seems to work for him/her. Cognitive and Behavioral Theory says that psychological problems occur because of medical or physiological problems {Cognitive} or that problems can be attributed to his/her reaction, or action, to environmental influences {Behavioral}.

To provide another perspective of theory comparison associated with the three things mentioned I will list them separately with the theories I believe best corresponds to each:
1}. Our family of origin: Psychoanalytic; Cognitive Behavioral
2} Our own thoughts and feelings; Cognitive Behavioral; Psychoanalytic; Adlerian and Existentialist.
3} What the world, or society, teaches us: Cognitive Behavioral; Psychoanalytic

My increased relationship with God has empowered me to utilize my psychological education and training with spiritual education and training. In this way, God has given me the greatest opportunity to fulfill his greatest commission, "to be fishers of men." With that, I will discuss Christian Therapy.

There are many therapists who practice Christian Therapy and are often times referred to as "Faith Based Counseling." What I have discovered is that Faith Based Counseling is called Faith Based due to receiving Government assistance. It should not be assumed that this is always the case. A therapist or agency that uses the word "Faith" maybe using it this way so not to offend individuals of a particular denomination or want to be identified, or associated with, a particular denomination. It could also be assumed that these agencies may incorporate many different belief systems. Just as there are different names for the practice of Christian Therapy, there are many ways to practice it as well. Probably a person who has the distinction known as clergy {minister, pastor etc.} or "person of the cloth" would be the most recognizable, or first thought. I will use the word "clergy" throughout for clarity and not to seem biased.

I would describe clergy as a person who has a degree from a Christian, or Seminary type, University of higher education that focuses on the Church and the bible. Individuals who have graduated from those institutions are typically members of a particular church, or have relatives that are in a ministry of some sort and have attended the same University. Most of these Universities are associated with a particular denomination such as Baptist, Nazarene, Catholic, Lutheran etc. However there are some Universities that do not associate themselves with a denomination such as, Light University {www.acc.org.} in Virginia and Destiny University in Winter Haven, FL. {a co-worker of mine is about to graduate with a Doctorate in Theology} etc. I do not have any expert knowledge concerning these Universities, therefore I can not offer any details about the education associated with these and similar Universities. However, believe it would be safe to assume that those Universities associated with a denomination, educate from that particular denominations beliefs and values and those unaffiliated Universities have what is termed an "eclectic" education, in other words, teaches from different Christian perspectives.

The non-denominational Universities may be more beneficial to individuals who may not be Christian, or those who may be interested in help from a Christian perspective. Also, these therapists may be best appropriate for those individuals who have fallen out of the Church or feel they have been "forgotten", or "burned" by religion. Christian Therapy is primarily done by a

Pastor or Minister, however there are some denominations that have therapists on staff and this is part of their ministry. For example, at the church our family attends we have a therapist and he is licensed with a degree. The persons who do therapy in a church setting often practice with little or no charge for services. The difference is made up with donations or is part of a ministry where a tithing is taken up.

Christian therapy is also done within agencies as well. Some have directors who are ordained clergy, have a degree, or have a license to do therapy. However, clergy does not have a license to do therapy, they also can not charge for their services. In the area where I live, I know of at least four agencies that are Christian focused. I work part time at one of these and we offer income based fees, insurance billing and no fee for services. At the facility where I work at we have five therapists including myself.

As I mentioned earlier, most clients associated with a Christina based agency, pay for their services without the benefit of insurance coverage. This is how the income based fee for services is applied. This is the same as mentioned earlier for the Community mental Health agencies. The most important difference is that Community agencies are provided grant money from the Government, whereas Christian agencies do not receive Government funds therefore, making for a better environment to conduct therapy.

Therapy with a Christian therapist is the same as with any other therapist. We are bound by the same ethical guidelines such as, empathy, unbiased opinions, unconditional love and professionalism and we apply the same techniques and therapeutic processes as all therapists do. There are two distinct differences. One is that we utilize the Bible within our therapeutic strategy and the other one is Gods' teachings through Jesus to help facilitate change within our clients. Unlike most psychologists who are predominantly non believers due to the liberal arts training they receive and the social implications for mentioning God in a school setting, we believe that all things are created and designed by God and that all things are to be used for his glory and his purpose. We believe the Bible to be the inspired word of God and thus the blueprint for living our lives. I recall in my college studies there was no mention of Christianity only of a higher power {this could be anything a person could think of!}. Sadly, there are many Christians as well as denominations that do not believe in therapy. I believe the reasons for this are many. However, there are two that have been mentioned to me by others. The first, most psychologists do not acknowledge God therefore, therapy must be satanic. Second, many Christians believe that God is the ultimate healer. God is the ultimate healer, look at all the miracles he performed in the Bible and is still doing today. I too, believe that God is the ultimate healer. I also believe that God works through people in healing others, such as Doctors and Dentists. I believe that therapists are utilized in the same manner. The Christian therapist helps to facilitate change for the individual just like any other therapist. You may be wondering how is facilitating change with the client different with Christian therapy?

There are two distinct possibilities for change. First, a person needs to accept the reality that he/she is a sinner. Second, he/she needs to understand that God has created them for a specific purpose. Let's look at these separately.

What does it mean that he/she is a sinner? Well, I believe there are two ways to answer this question. First, there is no way that we can be aware of doing the right thing all of the time due to many different things such as, personal desires {wishes}, emotional reactions, individual beliefs and values, differences in thinking and relating to others etc. All we have to do is watch the news and we can hear about bad things being done and realize that sin is prevalent in the world. Second, we were born into sin as a result of Adam and Eves' decision as well as them being tempted by the serpent to do what God specifically told them not to do. I do not know this for sure, but I believe that Gods' gift of free will may have also contributed to the fall of man. I mentioned free will because we can either choose to follow God, or we can choose not to. However, God is always there, possibly through our conscience, to give us thoughts of doubt or worry concerning things we have done or decisions we have made. It is impossible for any human being to be perfect. In other words, we can not know everything and do everything because of our limitations. Even with knowledge, it is impossible due to the inability to predict what a person will do. However, with focus on what God says and teaches, we can begin to internally process things in this way. By doing so, we can dramatically reduce the tendency to do the wrong thing.

You may be wondering, if the Christian therapist relies heavily on Gods' word and teachings, how does psychological theory apply? I believe that all things have been designed and created by God. With that, since God designed all of us humans for a specific purpose, then we are responsible for using Gods' given blessings not for our benefit, but for him and others. Due to our sinful nature and God given free will, we often times rely on our own understanding instead of Gods' will and desires for us. Because of our nature and our ability to make our own decisions, we are influenced by what we can see, hear, touch, taste, smell as well as our imagination. With that, I believe that the psychological theories we have are beneficial in helping us to understand our God given purpose and to explore those things that keep us from experiencing God. Again, because of our sinful nature, selfishness and pressure from society, we tend to take what God has given us and use it for our benefit and not necessarily for his.

Summary

We can easily pick up a phone book and find several practitioners and facilities that provide therapeutic services. We can also get information from friends, relatives and physicians concerning where to obtain services. However, none of these resources provide information concerning what therapy is and more specifically, what kind of therapy is utilized except for family, substance abuse, marital etc. It is up to the individual to inquire about the information discussed within this book. But how can an individual ask questions to receive the kind of therapy they need if they do not have some knowledge concerning what therapy is and which methods are utilized within therapy?

I began by discussing the types of therapy that are offered with information regarding where an individual might expect to receive such kinds of therapy. I also explained how each kind of therapy is conducted and under what circumstances an individual may be exposed to a specific kind of therapy. I also described the kind of environment in which each type of therapy is utilized. Though I did mention long term and short term therapies and indicated that insurance providers are mostly responsible for determining this. Length of treatment is solely based upon the individual whom is receiving therapy. Professionally I have provided services for as little as two months and as long as 15 months (this person is in therapy as of the writing of this book). Another important factor in the length of treatment is the individual's diagnosis and the individual's level of commitment to therapy is also very important.

The second part of the book dealt with the kinds of therapy that are utilized in an effort to help individuals. I did not go into great detail about them, which was not the focus of this book, but to provide a general knowledge of what is practiced so that you, the reader, would have some degree of insight. Whether it be to educate yourself, or to discover which kind of therapy would work best for you. In any case, I felt that individuals should have some degree of knowledge concerning the different kinds of therapeutic approaches that are available and what an individual could expect from it. However, the therapies discussed within these pages were not exhaustive rather it provided a general overview, again the purpose behind writing this book. As previously mentioned, most therapies overlap. With that a therapist will rely, or should rely, on each and every therapeutic technique to provide the best treatment for the individual with whom they are working with. Therapy should be conducted with the interest of the individual in mind and not what others believe is the best for him/her.

If you or someone you know has been to therapy and the results were a disaster, it is important to keep in mind that just as there are personality conflicts and differences of opinion in the general public, we therapists experience the same. In this event, locate a therapist and ask him/her questions such as their qualifications, education and training background as well as their work experiences. With these questions and the information contained within the pages of this book you should be comfortable with the therapist and the methods he/she utilizes. Also remember that it takes two individuals to make a relationship and if you or someone else's relationship with a therapist was not satisfactory, perhaps it was a result of a personality conflict, or one of you was not fully committed to the therapeutic process.

I sincerely hope that this book has not only provided you with good information, but has also dispelled some of the myths concerning therapy. Regardless of what has been portrayed within the media, or told by others, we therapists have a desire to help others become better individuals, not just for themselves but, for our society as a whole. I hope that I have decreased some anxieties, or apprehensions about seeking therapeutic intervention. I believe that in order for individuals to understand the benefits of receiving any kind of service, they should have available to them some information regarding that service. If you are going to purchase a home, lets say, wouldn't you want to know its' assets and liabilities? How about a car? Wouldn't you want to know its' maintenance history? How it was maintained and by whom? It should be the same for an individual and their mental health, because nothing is more important than a person!! One last question: Do you know what therapy is?

Thank you for taking the time to read this book. It has been a pleasure for me to provide this information to you. I hope you receive as much in reading it as I have in writing it. God Bless!

Acknowledgements

The thought of writing a book had been in the back of my mind for many years. As I progressed through my profession I had many different topics that were of interest. Most were about specific psychological disorders. As I discovered there were many books written on this subject and frankly they were very dry, even for someone who understood the subject matter.

It was not until three years later that I was led to write "What is Therapy?" As I progressed with the writing, and explained to others what I was writing, they became interested and wanted to see the manuscript as it developed. Writing is the easy part. It is the grammar, sentence structure and content that makes a great and interesting book. Because I am extremely limited in these areas, I asked some dear friends, peers and family to address these areas as well as readability. I am so blessed to have had the following individuals involved in this project with me and I sincerely hope that they will participate again!

First and foremost I would like to thank my Heavenly Father, God, for the gift of therapy and the knowledge to work and for Him using me for His glory and purpose!!

Laura Warfel for her encouragement and willingness to read the manuscript, as well as provide me with her wisdom as a writer herself. Laura has taught writing at the College level and has written in several publications. I thank her for her attention to detail and in assisting me with keeping my readers focus.

Kent Maddox LCSW for his support and encouragement. He also was instrumental in assisting with editing and content of the therapies. Kent has had 20 years experience as a therapist/ director of Caring Counseling Ministries.

Gary Reed LCPC for his support, encouragement and attention to content and accuracy. Gary has worked as a Christian

Therapist, in a Supervisor role for therapists seeking licensure. Currently Gary works with a major insurance company where he deals with therapy over the telephone.

My Mother for her contribution to content, grammar and sentence structure and her enthusiastic support and encouragement!

And last, but certainly not least, my Family. In particular my wife Marcia, for exhaustively editing the words, sentence structure and flow from a man that suffers from Dyslexia and does not know the difference between a run on sentence and a fragment! Our children, Makayla and Logan, for "allowing" me time to work during nap time and movie time.